LIFE'S LITTLE
ZUCCHINI COOKBOOK:

101 Zucchini Recipes

by Joan Bestwick

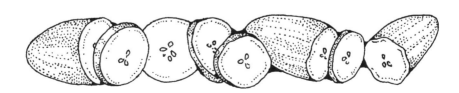

Life's Little Zucchini Cookbook
101 Zucchini Recipes
by Joan Bestwick

Copyright 1997
by Avery Color Studios, Inc.
ISBN# 0-932212-94-8
Library of Congress Card #97-070281
First Edition June 1997
Reprinted September 1999

Published by
Avery Color Studios, Inc.
Gwinn, Michigan 49841

Proudly printed in U.S.A.

Table of Contents

This cookbook is dedicated to:

My husband Greg who has always encouraged me and inspires me;

My son Michael who tried to have patience to let me write;

My parents Mary Anne and Victor who taught me determination and dreams;

To God and Jesus Christ, who give me everything I need;

My forever friend Karen who loves me no matter what and never lets me stray;

My sister Jean who is always there;

My brother John to whom I tell my secrets and dreams;

My two friends Lavern and Victoria who allow me to grow and change;

I love all of you. Thank you.

Never give up on anybody. Miracles happen everyday.

*H*ello, my name is Joanie and I really enjoyed writing this book. After working for years, first in home health nursing and then switching over to social work as a strong client advocate and state public speaker in the Domestic Violence Movement, I got married and was blessed with a miracle baby. I am now a stay-at-home mom who cares for one very active child.

This book was hard to write in a sense because I usually cook "off the cuff." A dab of this, a dash of that and a taste test to see if anything is missing. If creativity is an expression of one's soul, as they say, then the kitchen is the one area in your home you can express yourself endlessly. My husband and I both enjoy cooking and spend a lot of time exploring and experimenting with food.

Feel free to adjust these recipes to your taste; be creative with them. I love fresh herbs and vegetables and try to use a combination of both when I cook and allow the flavors to meld. The aroma that fills the home warms the heart and with the table set, we find much to thank the Lord for before we eat.

Is there another cookbook in my future? Maybe! More creativity? Definitely!! Thank you for your interest in my book and I pray you enjoy it. Live each day to the fullest and learn to cook and love the little things in life. May you always have a smile on your face and a prayer in your heart.

*T*he most often-heard question during the vegetable harvest time is "What do I do with all this zucchini?" One plant alone, if pollinated by the busy bees, can produce enough zucchini to feed your neighborhood! If you don't want your neighbors to go into hiding, this cookbook can introduce them to many new ways to serve zucchini. Have a zucchini party starting with hors d'oeuvres, soup, a main dish and dessert. Dazzle them with your culinary creativity. You'll have them begging to take your abundant supply of zucchini home.

If you are one of those people who grow zucchini to the size of Noah's Ark and then try to pass it off, scaring the receiver into cardiac arrest, try reverse psychology. Pick it while it's young and tender, when you can do more with it and it is used up faster. If you are stuck with Noah's Ark, try a meal such as: a soup of zucchini, followed by meatloaf, adding a cup of shredded zucchini to your mixture. Then chop it, sauté it in butter and garlic or roll it in bread crumbs and parmesan cheese and fry it. While you are preparing this meal, whip up the nutritious zucchini bread (2 or 3 batches) for the next day's breakfast, but use muffin tins instead of loaf pans. This way your little darlings can take the muffins off to school and pass them out to friends and teachers and your husband can put them out by the coffee pot at work. Then follow your dinner with one of the delicious desserts. For example, add a cup of shredded zucchini for mouth-watering moist brownies. Presto! Noah's Ark is gone. The stress of that big green monster in your refrigerator is gone, and you feel good because you fed your family a nutritious meal and they had no idea you hid this vegetable in their food.

With people so health conscious today, zucchini is that non-fat little green guy that fits easily in the refrigerator. It is very versatile and can be added some way, somehow, to most of your dishes. It is great raw with dip, and it can be used in place of cucumbers, for that person who gets that unbearable cucumber burp syndrome. For the best nutritious benefits, leave the peel on, for that is where the majority of the nutrition is. I know by purchasing this book you have made a great step toward zucchini independence. People will come to you for zucchini advice, and you will have all the answers to the most often-heard question, "What do I do with all this zucchini?" Enjoy and God bless.

Joanie

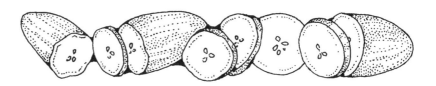

Tips for Zucchini

 Dehydrating zucchini: Wash, peel and grate the zucchini and place on a paper towel. Place another paper towel on top and press to remove excess moisture. Then spread the zucchini on the dehydrator trays and dry for 8 to 10 hours. Store in a air-tight glass container or heavy plastic bags.

 Quick grated zucchini: Place unpeeled chunks of zucchini in a blender and cover with water. Blend on chop for 3 to 5 seconds and drain, pressing out as much water as possible, then pat with a paper towel to absorb the remaining moisture.

 Zucchini:

1/2 cup of sliced zucchini has 14 calories and 0.1 gram of fat.

1 pound = 2 cups

1 – 1-1/4 pounds = 1 pint

 Slices: Use small young squash with tender skin. Wash and cut in 1/2 inch slices and blanch in boiling water for 3 minutes, cool promptly in cold water, drain, package and freeze.

Grated: Use this for baking. Use young tender squash, wash, grate or shred, then in small quantities, blanch for 1 to 2 minutes, until translucent. Cool in ice water and drain. Freeze in sealed containers. Drain liquid when thawed before use.

 Cubed: You can use any size zucchini for this; wash, cut in half, and remove the seeds if necessary. Cut into cubes, blanch for 2 to 3 minutes, and cool in cold water. Drain well and pack in containers. Freeze.

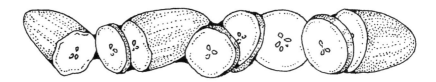

APPETIZERS
and
WHAT NOT

Focus on making things better, not bigger.

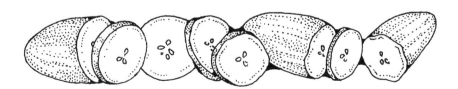

Pizza Zucchini Appetizers

1 medium zucchini, sliced 1/2 inch thick
1/3 cup canned tomato sauce
2 ounces cooked ground sausage
1/4 to 1/2 cup shredded mozzarella cheese
1 tablespoon grated parmesan cheese
1/4 teaspoon dried basil
1/4 teaspoon crushed red pepper

Spray a non-stick cookie sheet with vegetable spray, then place the zucchini slices (about 16) on the sheet. Spread each slice with tomato sauce, top with cooked sausage, then sprinkle with both cheeses, basil and pepper. Broil 3 to 4 inches from heat for about 4 to 5 minutes or until cheese melts.

Dutch Relish

4 cups diced zucchini
1 cup vinegar
1 teaspoon salt
1/2 cup sugar
1/4 cup prepared horseradish

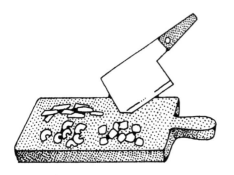

In a medium enamel or stainless steel pan, mix all ingredients. Bring to a boil, cool completely, and drain. Makes 4 cups. Keeps in the refrigerator. This is a good relish for wild game.

Zucchini Relish

10 cups zucchini, ground
4 cups ground onion
5 tablespoons salt

Cover with water and soak for 5 hours or overnight.

In a stainless steel pot, bring the following ingredients to a boil.

1 cup green pepper, chopped
4 cups white sugar
2-1/2 cups vinegar
2 teaspoons turmeric
2 tablespoons cornstarch
1 - 4 oz. can of pimentos, chopped
1 teaspoon nutmeg
2 teaspoons celery seed
1/2 teaspoon pepper

Combine with drained zucchini mixture and simmer for 1/2 hour, then put in hot jars and seal.

Zucchini Relish Tartar Sauce

1/2 cup zucchini relish
1 cup salad dressing
2 to 3 tablespoons lemon juice

Mix well in a small bowl.

Zucchini Marmalade

4 cups zucchini, grated
1/2 cup lemon juice
grated orange peel from 4 medium oranges
2 cups water
1 package pectin
5 cups sugar

In a heavy pan combine the first four ingredients and boil until mixture is tender and clear, about 10 minutes, stirring occasionally so it does not burn. Add pectin and bring back to a boil. Add sugar and bring to a hard rolling boil that can't be stirred down, stirring constantly for 2 minutes. Remove from heat and stir for 5 minutes. Place into sterilized jars and seal.

Zucchini Jam

6 cups zucchini, peeled and diced
Lemon juice from two lemons
1 teaspoon grated lemon peel
1 - 15 oz. can crushed pineapple
1 box pectin
5 cups sugar
1 tablespoon cinnamon

Mix first four ingredients in a heavy pan and boil for 15 minutes. Add box of pectin and mix well. Bring the mixture back to a boil, add the sugar and cinnamon and boil for one more minute, stirring constantly so as not to burn. Remove from heat and place in sterilized jars and seal.

Zucchini "Watermelon" Pickles

3 pounds zucchini
4 tablespoons alum
3 quarts water
Ice cubes

Peel zucchini and cut into chunks. In a large kettle, heat, but do not boil, the alum and 3 quarts water. Place the zucchini in a large bowl, pour the liquid over it and cover with ice. Let stand for 2 hours. Drain well.

SYRUP:
8 cups sugar
4 cinnamon sticks
4 cups vinegar
4 teaspoons whole cloves
2 cups water
1 thinly sliced lemon

FOR SYRUP

In a large kettle combine ingredients and bring to a full boil. Pour over the zucchini and let stand overnight. The next day, bring the zucchini and syrup to a boil, boiling until the zucchini is transparent. Pack into sterilized jars and seal. At this time you can add a few drops of red food coloring for color.

SOUPS

Take charge of your attitude. Don't let someone else choose it for you.

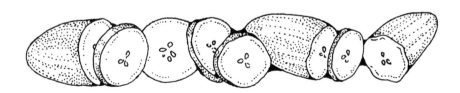

Zucchini Soup – Mexican Style

1 pound zucchini
1-1/2 quarts (6 cups) chicken stock
1/2 cup diced fresh onion
1 teaspoon salt (optional)
1/4 cup butter or margarine
2 tablespoons flour
1/2 teaspoon black pepper
dash cayenne pepper
2 egg yolks
1/2 cup heavy cream
1/4 cup crumbled crackers
ground nutmeg

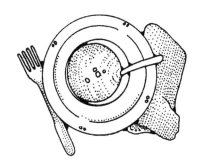

Wash and slice unpeeled squash. In a medium size heavy pan, add zucchini, 3 cups chicken stock, onion and salt. Cover pan and cook 30 minutes or until squash falls apart. Mash squash through a sieve, and return to stock. Add remaining stock to pan. In another medium pan melt butter over medium heat, then add flour using a whisk. Stir until slightly browned. Gradually add stock and squash mixture and black pepper and cayenne to flour mixture. Cook over medium heat until soup has slightly thickened, about 5-7 minutes. Blend egg yolks with cream and crackers and stir into hot soup. Serve hot with a dash of nutmeg.

Quick Italian Beef & Vegetable Soup

1 pound ground beef (or turkey, or pork)   *1 LARGE ONION*
4 large clove garlic, crushed
salt and pepper, to taste
2 cans (13-3/4 to 14-1/2 ounce) beef broth
1 can (12-14 ounce) Italian-style stewed tomatoes, broken up
1 cup carrots sliced 1/4 inch thick
1 can (15-19 ounce) Great Northern beans, rinsed and drained
3 medium zucchini, chopped in small pieces
2 cups torn spinach leaves.

SAUTE ONION
In a large soup pot over medium heat, add ground meat and garlic. Brown, breaking up into small crumbs. Drain fat. Add salt and pepper, broth, tomatoes,

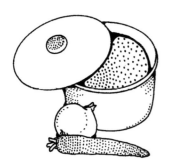

carrots and bring to a boil. Reduce heat. Simmer uncovered for 10 minutes. Stir in beans and add zucchini; cook 4 to 5 minutes longer or until zucchini is crisp/tender. Remove from heat; stir in spinach. Serves 4.

Chilled Zucchini Soup

3 small zucchini, cubed
1 small green pepper, chopped
6 green onions, sliced diagonally
2-1/4 cups chicken broth
1 cup milk
pinch of ground red pepper

In a large skillet, combine the zucchini, green pepper, onions and 2 tablespoons broth. Cover and cook over medium-low heat about 10 minutes, or until the vegetables are tender, stirring occasionally. If necessary, add more broth during cooking to prevent vegetables from browning. Transfer the vegetable mixture to a blender or food processor. Blend until smooth, adding remaining broth. Return mixture to skillet. Cover and bring to boil. Reduce heat. Simmer 5 minutes. Remove from heat and stir in milk and red pepper. Cover and chill in refrigerator for at least 1 hour. Serves four.

Zucchini Soup

2 tablespoons olive oil
4 medium zucchini, peeled and diced
1 medium onion, sliced thin
1 pound canned tomatoes
1/2 cup cooked rice or 1/2 cup cooked macaroni
2 tablespoons butter

In a soup pot, over medium heat, warm the olive oil. Add the zucchini and onion and sauté until tender. Add tomatoes, pasta or rice and butter. Season with salt and pepper to taste. Heat through and serve. Water may be added for a thinner soup.

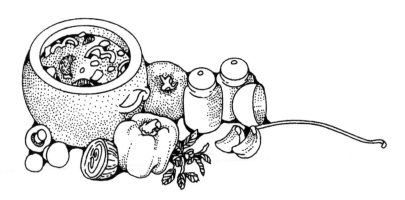

Lo-Cal Zucchini Soup

1 large or 2 small zucchini, peeled and diced
1 large onion or several small green onions, sliced
2 carrots, sliced
2 stalks celery, sliced in 1/2 inch slices
1 can tomatoes (about 1 pint) (FRESH TOMATOES)
3 cups ~~water~~ (NON-FAT VEG. BROTH)
Herbs and seasonings to taste

In a soup kettle, cook zucchini and carrots in one cup of water until barely tender. Add other ingredients cooking over low heat until vegetables are tender. Season to your liking; garlic salt, herb salt or fresh chopped herbs taste the best. This soup will be thick like chili and is a meal in itself.

Apple and Zucchini Soup

1-1/2 cups chicken broth
1/2 cup unsweetened apple juice
1 small zucchini, sliced thin
1 small apple, cored and thinly sliced
2 green onions, sliced thin
1/2 teaspoon grated lemon peel
1/8 teaspoon ground nutmeg

In a medium saucepan, over medium to high heat, combine all ingredients. Bring to a boil and cover, reduce heat and simmer for about 3 minutes until apple and zucchini are crisp-tender. 4 servings.

SALADS

Live your life as an exclamation, not an explanation.

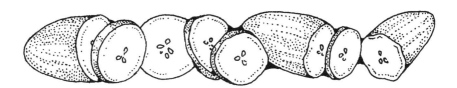

Zippy Zucchini Relish Salad

1/2 cup oil
1/4 cup vinegar
1 envelope (1/2 ounce) spaghetti sauce mix
1 teaspoon sugar
2 tablespoons chopped green onion
5 to 6 cups diced zucchini
1/2 cup chopped green pepper

In a medium bowl combine oil, vinegar, spaghetti sauce mix and sugar, mixing well. Add onion, zucchini and green pepper, and toss well until coated. Chill for 2 hours or more before serving. Makes approximately 6 cups.

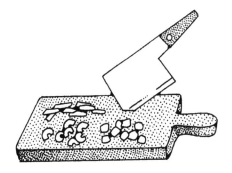

Zucchini Salad

4 small zucchini, sliced thin
4 to 6 Roma tomatoes, cut into wedges
1 small green pepper, sliced into strips
1/4 cups sliced green onions
1/4 cup fresh snipped parsley

DRESSING:
3/4 cup salad oil
1/4 cup vinegar
1 clove garlic, minced
1 teaspoon salt
1 teaspoon pepper

In a salad bowl, toss vegetables. Combine the dressing ingredients in a container, shaking until the ingredients are mixed well. Pour over vegetables, stirring to coat, and chill for several hours, stirring occasionally.

Sweet and Sour Zucchini Salad

1/8 cup wine vinegar
3/4 cup sugar
1 teaspoon salt
1/2 teaspoon pepper
1/3 cup salad oil
2/3 cup cider vinegar
1/2 cup chopped green pepper
1/2 cup sliced onion
1/2 cup sliced celery
5 small zucchini, sliced paper thin

In a bowl, combine vinegar, oil, sugar, salt and pepper and mix well. Pour over vegetables, mixing again. Marinate for 6 hours or overnight. Drain and serve. Makes 12 servings.

Zucchini Salad to Serve a Million

10 pounds zucchini, sliced thin
4 pounds tomatoes, quartered
4 pounds sliced onions
1 gallon salad oil
1-1/2 quarts vinegar
4 tablespoons prepared mustard
4 tablespoons salt
1 tablespoon pepper
1 tablespoon oregano

Combine all ingredients in a large crock. Let stand for seven days, turning daily. Serves millions!

Zucchini and Mint Salad

1 tablespoon and 1 teaspoon olive oil
4 cups thinly sliced zucchini
3 tablespoons minced fresh mint
1 garlic clove, crushed
1/2 teaspoon salt
1/4 teaspoon black pepper

In a large non-stick skillet over medium-high heat, add 2 teaspoons oil and 2 cups zucchini. Cook for 4 to 5 minutes stirring frequently until golden-brown. Drain with slotted spoon and place zucchini in a medium sized bowl. Repeat with the other 2 cups of zucchini. Add mint, garlic, salt, pepper and 2 teaspoons of olive oil. Toss to combine. Cover the bowl and refrigerate until chilled. Serves 4.

Zucchini and Carrot Salad with Cumin Dressing

✳ MAKE A FEW HOURS IN ADVANCE

1/2 *teaspoon ground cumin*

3 *2 tablespoons and 2 teaspoons mayonnaise*

2 *1 tablespoon chopped cilantro*

1 *tablespoon lime juice* , / TBS BALSAMIC VINEGAR

1/2 *teaspoon grated lime zest*

1/4 *teaspoon salt*

1/8 *teaspoon pepper*

2 *medium julienne sliced carrots* ✓ SWEET, FRESH CUT THIN

1 *medium julienne sliced zucchini*

1/2 LB SMALL SLICED TOMATOES

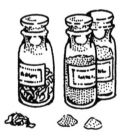

To prepare dressing: heat cumin over low heat in a small skillet, stirring frequently until fragrant, about 1 minute. In a small bowl add warm cumin, mayo, cilantro, juice, zest, salt and pepper. Mix well. In a medium bowl, combine carrots and zucchini and cover with dressing, tossing to mix. Serves 4.

PASTA and RICE

*Judge your success by the degree that you're
enjoying peace, health and love.*

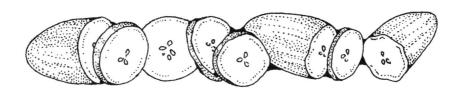

Bacon and Garlic Pasta

1 - 16 ounce package of pasta, your choice
1/2 pound sliced bacon, cut up in chunks
1 medium onion, chopped
4 to 6 cloves garlic, minced
2 to 3 medium zucchini, halved and sliced
1/2 teaspoon salt
3 tablespoons lemon juice
1/4 cup grated parmesan cheese

Cook pasta according to package directions. In a large skillet over medium heat, cook bacon until crisp. Remove the bacon with a slotted spoon and drain on a paper towel, discarding all but 2 tablespoons of drippings. Sauté onion and garlic in drippings, about 3 minutes. Add the zucchini and salt, cooking until tender, about 6 minutes. Drain pasta and add to the zucchini mixture. Add lemon juice and bacon and toss. Transfer to serving bowl and sprinkle with cheese. Serves 6 to 8.

Zucchini and Carrot Manicotti

12 manicotti shells, cooked as directed
1 - 15 ounce container ricotta cheese
1 cup coarsely shredded carrot
1 cup coarsely shredded zucchini
1/2 cup shredded mozzarella cheese
2 tablespoons chopped fresh parsley
2 teaspoons sugar
1 egg white slightly beaten
1 - 26 to 30 ounce jar spaghetti sauce
1/4 cup grated parmesan cheese

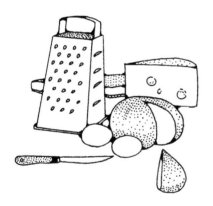

Preheat oven to 350°. In a bowl mix ricotta cheese, carrot, zucchini, mozzarella cheese, parsley, sugar and egg. Fill the cooked manicotti shells and place in a baking dish. Cover with spaghetti sauce and parmesan cheese and bake for 45 minutes.

Rosemary and Zucchini Pasta

1 tablespoon butter (" You Can't Believe")
3 garlic cloves, minced
2 cups sliced zucchini
2 cups sliced yellow summer squash
1 cup red bell pepper strips
1 cup canned crushed tomatoes
1/2 cup orange juice
1 tablespoon fresh rosemary leaves
2 teaspoons chicken bouillon granules
3 cups cooked pasta wheels, cooked as directed
1/4 cup chopped fresh parsley

In a large non-stick skillet, heat margarine over low heat. Add garlic to the margarine and cook for 5 minutes stirring often. Add zucchini, squash, pepper strips, tomatoes, orange juice, rosemary leaves and chicken bouillon granules. Stir to combine, reduce heat to low and simmer for 5 minutes or until vegetables are crisp-tender. Remove from heat, stir in pasta and sprinkle with parsley. Serves 4-6.

Orzo and Garlic Spring Vegetables

4-1/2 ounces uncooked orzo
1 tablespoon olive oil
2 tablespoons minced fresh ginger root
3 garlic cloves, crushed
2 cups sliced baby carrots
2 cups sliced baby zucchini
1 cup chopped red bell pepper
1 cup chopped yellow bell pepper
1 teaspoon chicken bouillon granules
   dissolved in 3/4 cup boiling water
1/8 teaspoon pepper

In a medium saucepan, bring 3 cups of water to a boil and stir in the orzo. Reduce heat to low and simmer for 8 to 10 minutes or until orzo is tender. Drain and set aside. In a large skillet heat oil, ginger and garlic, cooking over low heat for 5 minutes, stirring frequently. Increase heat to high and stir fry by adding vegetables and dissolved bouillon. Cook for 3 minutes, stirring continuously, until vegetables are crisp-tender. Add cooked orzo and pepper and mix well. Serves 6.

SIDE DISHES
with
CHEESE and EGGS

*Become the most positive and enthusiastic
person you know.*

Zucchini Custard

1 pound zucchini
4 eggs, lightly beaten
1 cup shredded cheddar cheese
1-1/2 cup milk, scalded
1 tablespoon butter
1 teaspoon salt
1/4 teaspoon paprika
1 teaspoon chopped green onion

Preheat oven to 350°. Cut zucchini into large chunks and place in a pan of boiling water. Cook until tender, drain and cut into bite size pieces. Combine all ingredients, mixing well, and pour into a greased casserole dish. Place the casserole dish in a baking pan, then add water to the baking pan. Bake for 50 to 60 minutes. Serves 6.

Zucchini Patties

5 medium zucchini
3 eggs
1 tablespoon grated parmesan cheese
1 clove of garlic, minced or mashed
2 tablespoons flour
1/2 cup finely chopped parsley
1 teaspoon salt
1 teaspoon pepper
1/2 cup olive oil or salad oil

Coarsely shred unpeeled zucchini and press out excess water. In a bowl combine all ingredients until well mixed. In a skillet over medium heat, heat a small amount of oil. Drop mixture by heaping tablespoons into hot oil and fry until browned. Serves 6.

Zucchini Pancakes

1 large zucchini, grated
1 egg
2 tablespoons flour
1/2 teaspoon baking powder
1 tablespoon sugar
1/2 teaspoon salt

Combine all ingredients and mix well. Add a small amount of oil or margarine to a skillet and heat. Pour small amounts of batter into the skillet and fry on each side until golden brown. 2 servings.

Herb Zucchini Frittata

2 small zucchini
1 teaspoon water
2 green onions, finely chopped
1 tablespoon fresh chopped basil
1-1/2 teaspoons fresh chopped parsley
4 to 6 eggs beaten with 2 tablespoons water
2 tablespoons grated parmesan cheese

Slice zucchini into 1/4 inch slices, then cut the slices into quarters. In an oven proof skillet, over medium-low heat, add water, zucchini and onions. Cook until vegetables are crisp-tender and drain. Add basil and parsley, then carefully

add the eggs. Cook over low heat until eggs begin to set. Using a spatula, lift the edges of the cooked egg to allow the uncooked mixture to flow underneath. Continue cooking until almost firm, but moist on top. Sprinkle with cheese, place under broiler and heat for about 1 minute or until the top is lightly browned and the mixture is set. Serves 4.

Zucchini Mold

6 to 7 zucchini, thinly sliced
1 carrot, finely chopped
1 medium onion, finely chopped
1/4 cup finely chopped fresh parsley
3 tablespoons butter
1/3 cup grated parmesan cheese
3 eggs, lightly beaten
1 cup basic white sauce

Melt butter in a skillet over medium heat. Cook the carrot, onion and parsley until the onion has browned. Add the zucchini and seasoning and cook gently for 10 to 15 minutes, until the zucchini is tender. Remove from heat and add cheese, eggs and white sauce. Place the mixture in a buttered oven proof mold and cover with a sheet of wax paper. Place the mold in a baking dish, fill the baking dish with hot water until it reaches half way up the side of the mold. Bake for 45 minutes at 300°. Serve hot. Serves 4.

Zucchini Herb Flan

2 teaspoons olive oil
4 cups grated zucchini
1 cup chopped onion
2 cloves minced garlic
2 teaspoons white wine vinegar
1/4 cup chopped fresh parsley
1 teaspoon chopped fresh thyme
1/2 teaspoon chopped fresh rosemary
1/4 teaspoon pepper
1 cup egg substitute
1/3 cup and 2 teaspoons flour
1/4 cup grated parmesan cheese

Preheat oven to 300°. Grease a 9" square baking pan. In a large non-stick baking pan over medium heat, add oil, zucchini, onion and garlic. Sauté for 12 minutes or until tender. Add vinegar and cook for 2 minutes, stirring frequently. Remove from heat and let cool slightly. Stir in herbs and seasonings. In a large bowl, whisk eggs, flour and cheese. Stir in zucchini mixture and transfer to baking pan. Bake for 30 to 35 minutes, until set. Serves 4.

Zucchini Quiche

1 - 10 inch pie crust
2 cups shredded Swiss cheese
2 tablespoons flour
1 large ripe tomato, peeled and sliced
1 medium zucchini, cut into thin slices
3 eggs, beaten well
1-1/2 cups milk or cream
1 teaspoon salt
1/2 teaspoon dry mustard
1/4 teaspoon pepper
1 tablespoon fresh chopped chives

Preheat oven to 350°. Prepare the pie crust. Combine Swiss cheese and flour and place on the bottom of the pie crust as the first layer. Top with tomato and zucchini slices. In a bowl, mix the eggs, milk or cream, seasoning and chives and pour over the vegetable slices. Bake for 50 minutes or until pie is puffy and brown. Serve immediately.

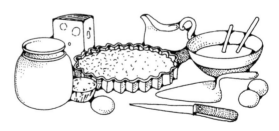

Zucchini Cheese Omelet

1 cup sliced zucchini
2 tablespoons butter or margarine
6 eggs
2 tablespoons water
1/4 teaspoon basil
1/4 teaspoon salt
dash of pepper
1/4 pound muenster, Monterey jack or mozzarella cheese

In a 10 inch skillet, sauté zucchini in butter until lightly browned. Beat eggs, water, basil, salt and pepper until well blended, and pour over squash.

Reduce heat to medium-low and cook without stirring until eggs are partially set. Lift edges with a spatula, tilting the skillet, to allow uncooked mixture to run underneath. While still moist, top with grated cheese and cover until cheese is partially melted. Slide omelet carefully out of pan onto serving dish, folding in half. Makes 4 servings.

MEAT
POULTRY
FISH

*Never deprive someone of hope; it might be
all they have.*

Zucchini Hot Pot

1 pound zucchini, sliced into 1/4 inch cubes
8 small onions, peeled
6 carrots, cut in 2 inch pieces
1 onion, chopped
1/4 cup butter or margarine
1 pound small wieners
1 can beef gravy
salt and pepper
fresh chopped parsley

Cook zucchini, carrots and whole onions in salted, boiling water until just tender. In a skillet sauté the chopped onion in butter until transparent, add wieners and brown. In a large pot, place the vegetables and wieners, and pour the gravy over the mixture. Cover and cook on medium heat until heated through. Place in a serving bowl and sprinkle with fresh parsley. Serves 6.

Summer Vegetable Stew

1 tablespoon vegetable or olive oil
1 large onion, sliced
3 medium zucchini, cut in 1/2 inch slices
2 yellow squash, cut in 1/2 inch slices
4 large tomatoes, peeled and cut into wedges
8 ounces green beans, cut and blanched
2 boiling potatoes, pared and cut into 1 inch
  cubes and cooked
1 teaspoon oregano
1 teaspoon salt
1/4 teaspoon pepper
2 cups cooked, shredded or cubed, beef, pork or chicken

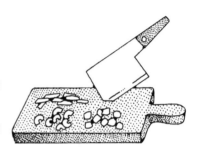

In a large skillet or soup pan, heat oil over medium-high heat. Add onion, stirring occasionally, about 5 minutes. Add the zucchini, yellow squash and tomatoes. Cook partially covered, allowing mixture to come to a simmer, reducing the heat to low. Simmer, partially covered and stirring occasionally, for 30 minutes or until vegetables are soft. Stir in beans, potatoes, oregano, salt, pepper and meat. Cook for 5 minutes.

Zucchini Sausage Boats

4 medium zucchini
1/4 pound bulk pork sausage
1/4 cup chopped onion
4 cups fine cracker crumbs
1 slightly beaten egg
1/2 cup grated parmesan cheese
1/2 teaspoon garlic powder
1/4 teaspoon salt
1/4 teaspoon ground pepper
1/4 teaspoon thyme

Preheat oven to 350°. In a large pot of salted boiling water, cook the whole zucchini until barely tender, 7 to 10 minutes. Remove from water, cool until able to touch. Cut squash in half lengthwise, scoop the squash out, being careful not to tear the skin of the zucchini, and mash. In a skillet over medium heat, brown the sausage, onion and seasonings, and drain the grease. Stir in the squash and all but 2 tablespoons of cheese, and mix well. Place zucchini shells in a baking pan and spoon in the meat mixture. Sprinkle with the remaining cheese and bake 25 to 30 minutes. Serves 4.

Italian Sausage Stir Fry

1 pound Italian sausage, any flavor
1/3 cup chopped onion
2 cups Roma tomatoes, chopped
4 cups julienne sliced zucchini
1/4 teaspoon Italian seasoning
salt and pepper to taste
fresh grated parmesan cheese

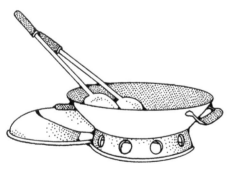

Crumble sausage from casing and place in a large skillet. Over medium-high heat, slightly brown the sausage and onion, draining the grease when cooked. Add the rest of the ingredients except the cheese and cook for 5 minutes, stirring often. Serves 4.

Leftover Pot Roast Greek Stew

2 teaspoons vegetable oil
1 large onion, chopped
3 medium zucchini (approximately 6 cups), cut into cubes
1 tablespoon minced garlic
1 - 15 ounce can tomato sauce
1/4 cup water
1/2 teaspoon cinnamon
1/2 teaspoon oregano
2-1/3 cups shredded pot roast

Heat the oil in a large non-stick skillet and sauté the onion for 2 minutes. Add the zucchini and garlic and sauté for 6 to 7 minutes. Stir in the tomato sauce, water, onion and seasonings and bring to a boil. Reduce the heat and simmer for 4 to 5 minutes, until slightly thickened. Stir in the pot roast and cook for another 2 to 3 minutes until hot. Serves 4.

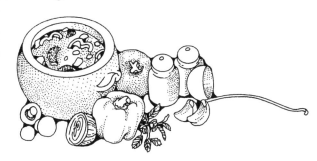

Zucchini Meatloaf

2 pounds ground beef
2 cups coarsely grated zucchini
1 cup dry Italian seasoned bread crumbs
1/2 cup grated parmesan cheese
1 tablespoon chopped parsley
1 small onion, chopped
1/2 package onion soup mix
1 cup milk
2 eggs
1/4 cup ketchup
1/2 teaspoon garlic powder

Preheat oven to 350°. Combine all ingredients in a large mixing bowl by hand, mixing well. Place meat mixture in a bread loaf pan. Bake for 1 hour. This can also be done in a crock pot on low for 2 to 4 hours depending on the crock pot size.

Zucchini Lasagna

4 large zucchini, cut lengthwise into 1/4 inch strips
2 tablespoons salad oil
2 cloves of garlic, minced
1/2 cup chopped onion
1 pound ground beef
2 cups diced tomatoes
1/2 cup sliced mushrooms
1-1/2 teaspoons oregano
1/4 teaspoon thyme
1 teaspoon basil
salt and pepper
8 ounces mozzarella cheese, sliced
1 cup grated parmesan cheese

Preheat oven to 350°. In a large skillet, sauté zucchini, onion and garlic in oil until vegetables are tender but firm. Remove the vegetables, and brown the meat in the same pan. When the meat is browned, add the tomatoes, tomato paste, mushrooms, herbs, salt and pepper. Simmer, uncovered 1-1/2 hours. In a greased baking dish, place 1/2 of the zucchini, topping it with 1/2 of the mozzarella cheese, and layering 1/2 of the meat mixture. Repeat the layers and top with parmesan cheese. Bake for 30 minutes. Serves 6.

Italian Beef Stir Fry

1 pound lean steak, 1/8 to 1/4 inch thick
2 cloves of garlic, crushed
1 tablespoon olive oil
2 small zucchini, thinly sliced
1 cup cherry tomato halves
1/4 cup reduced calorie Italian salad dressing
2 cups hot, cooked spaghetti
1 tablespoon grated parmesan cheese

Cut steak crosswise, into 1 inch wide strips, then cut each strip in half. In a large non-stick skillet over medium heat, add oil and garlic and heat for 1 minute. Add half of the beef strips at a time, stir frying for 1 to 1-1/2 minutes. Season with salt and pepper and remove from pan, keeping the meat warm. Add

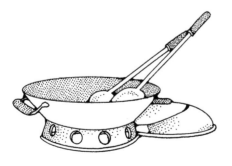

zucchini to skillet and stir fry 2 to 3 minutes or until crisp-tender. Return the beef to the skillet with the tomato halves and dressing. Heat through. Serve over hot pasta and sprinkle with cheese. Makes 4 servings.

Beef and Zucchini Bake

2 cups sliced zucchini
1/2 pound ground beef
1/4 cup rice, uncooked
1 - 16 ounce can tomatoes
1/4 cup diced green onion
1-1/2 teaspoons salt
1 teaspoon garlic powder
pepper to taste
1/4 cup Italian bread crumbs
2 cheese slices, any flavor

Preheat oven to 375°. In a medium size skillet, brown the meat, onion and seasoning. Add the zucchini, rice and tomatoes, mixing well. Place in a 2 quart casserole dish and top with bread crumbs. Bake for 45 minutes or until rice is tender. Top with cheese and place in oven until cheese melts. Serves 4.

Pasta with Zucchini Beef Sauce

1 pound ground meat, browned
1 garlic clove, crushed
1 tablespoon Italian seasoning
2 bay leaves
1 large can or jar spaghetti sauce
1 green pepper, diced
1 or 2 cans mushrooms
salt and pepper to taste
1/4 cup fresh parsley, chopped
1 pound sliced or cubed zucchini
4 to 6 tomatoes, cubed

Place all ingredients in a crock pot set on low heat. Mix well and cover for 4 to 6 hours, stirring occasionally. Remove bay leaves before serving. Serve over pasta. 4 servings.

Mexican Zucchini and Hamburger

2 pounds hamburger
4 medium zucchini, cut in one inch pieces
1 medium onion, chopped
3 cloves garlic, crushed
2 teaspoons cilantro, chopped
salt and pepper to taste
1 large can tomatoes (1 pound - 13 ounces)
1 large can corn (1 pound - 4 ounces)
oil

Brown hamburger in a skillet and drain the grease. In a separate skillet, sauté the zucchini and onion in a small amount of oil until tender. Add the zucchini and onion, seasoning, tomatoes and corn to hamburger and mix well. Cover and simmer for 30 minutes. Serves 6.

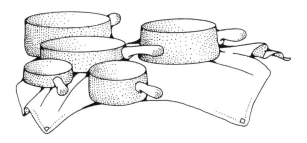

Zucchini Casserole

1 pound ground beef, turkey or pork
1 medium onion, chopped
3 - 8 ounce cans tomato sauce
1/4 teaspoon oregano
1/8 teaspoon garlic salt
1/4 teaspoon basil
1/2 teaspoon salt
1/2 teaspoon pepper
4 to 5 medium zucchini
1/4 cup grated parmesan cheese

In a skillet or crock pot, brown the ground meat and drain the grease. Add onion, tomato sauce, seasoning and herbs and mix. If using a crock pot, cook mixture on low for 4 to 5 hours, if using a skillet, cook for 1 hour. While this is cooking, cook the whole zucchini in a pan of salted, boiling water for 15 minutes or until barely tender. Cut lengthwise in half. Pour meat mixture into a greased baking dish and arrange zucchini halves, cut side up, on top of the meat mixture. Sprinkle with cheese and bake at 350°F for 30 to 45 minutes. Makes 4 to 5 servings. The prepared casserole can be refrigerated and baked the next day if desired.

Stuffed Zucchini

2 large zucchini, ends trimmed
1/2 pound ground beef
1/3 cup onion, chopped
1 large clove garlic, minced
1 teaspoon oregano
2 tablespoons olive oil
1/2 cup grated cheddar cheese
1 can tomato soup
1/4 cup grated parmesan cheese

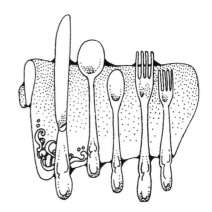

Preheat oven to 350°. Place zucchini in a pan of boiling water and boil for 5 minutes. Remove, cool, cut lengthwise and scoop out the center. Chop the pulp and set aside. In a large skillet over medium heat, brown the ground beef. Remove the ground beef and using the same skillet, sauté the onion, garlic and oregano in olive oil until tender. Place the ground beef back into the pan, adding the zucchini pulp, cheddar cheese and 1/4 can of tomato soup. Mix well and add the parmesan cheese. Place the zucchini shells in a shallow baking dish. Fill the hollow centers with the meat mixture, pour the remaining soup over top and sprinkle with more parmesan cheese. Cover and bake for 40 minutes, uncover and bake 5 more minutes.

Chicken Zucchini Casserole

4 cups cooked, cubed chicken or turkey
6 cups unpeeled, diced zucchini
1 cup onion, diced
1 cup shredded carrot
1 - 10-1/2 ounce can cream of chicken
  soup undiluted
1 8 ounce container of sour cream
1/8 teaspoon garlic powder
1 package chicken flavor stuffing mix
1/2 cup butter
1 cup cheddar cheese, grated

Preheat oven to 350°. In a medium saucepan, combine the zucchini and onion, adding enough water to cover. Bring to a boil for 5 minutes, drain and cool. In a large bowl, combine soup, sour cream and garlic powder, mixing well. Add the carrots, zucchini, onion and chicken to the soup mixture and place in a 9 x 13 inch greased baking dish. Melt butter in a medium skillet, add the stuffing and seasoning packet and toss well. Place stuffing over casserole and top with cheese. Bake for 1 hour or until golden brown. Serves 6 to 8.

Vegetable Chicken Fajitas

8 - 8-inch flour tortillas

—

1/4 cup lime juice
1 tablespoon olive oil
2 teaspoons chili powder, to taste
2 teaspoons minced garlic

In a small bowl combine the above ingredients, mixing well. Use this to marinate the following ingredients for 10 minutes.

4 - 4 ounce boneless, skinless chicken breasts
2 red bell peppers, quartered
2 small zucchini, chopped

After marinating, cook in a non-stick pan, over medium-high heat until chicken is fully cooked. Take a flour tortilla and fill with chicken mixture. Chopped tomatoes, avocado slices, chopped cilantro, sour cream or salsa can be added if desired.

Sweet and Sour Zucchini

2 tablespoons olive oil
1/2 pound thinly sliced chicken or pork
1/2 green pepper, thinly sliced
1/2 red pepper, thinly sliced
1 bunch green onions, sliced
1/2 box frozen pea pods (optional)
1 small can sliced water chestnuts
1 small can pineapple chunks, drained
2 small zucchini, sliced thin
1 package sweet and sour mix
maraschino cherries

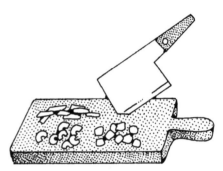

Heat oil in a large skillet or wok. Add meat, stirring frequently until no longer pink. Remove from pan and drain. Add vegetables to the pan, stirring frequently until tender but still crisp. While vegetables are cooking, prepare the package of sweet and sour mix according to directions. When the vegetables are ready, add the meat, sweet and sour mix and fruit, stirring until hot. Serve over rice.

Basil Chicken over Rice

2 cups brown rice, cooked
splash of olive oil
2 boneless, skinless chicken breasts, halved
2 teaspoons olive oil
1 cup onion, thinly sliced
1 small zucchini, sliced
1 clove garlic, minced
2 tablespoons chopped fresh basil
fresh ground pepper to taste

Warm the oil in a large non-stick skillet. Add the chicken and cook over medium-high heat for 5 to 6 minutes, until browned on both sides. Remove the chicken and cool the pan slightly. Add the onion, zucchini, garlic, basil and pepper to the pan, stirring to mix. Place the chicken on top of the vegetable mixture and cover. Cook over medium-low heat for 5 to 8 minutes, until the zucchini is translucent, the onions begin to brown and the chicken is cooked. Serve over rice.

Lemon Spring Veggie Fish

4 new potatoes, thinly sliced
1 tablespoon butter
2 carrots, thinly sliced
4 - 4 ounce cod or whitefish fillets
2 small zucchini, sliced
1 small onion, thinly sliced
1 tablespoon fresh dill, chopped
1/4 cup lemon juice

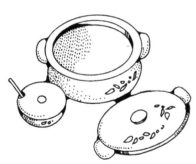

Preheat oven to 350°. In a small saucepan, cook the new potatoes in water until tender. In a medium skillet, over medium-high heat, melt the butter. Add the carrots and cook for 1 to 2 minutes, add the zucchini and onion and cook for another 2 to 3 minutes or until vegetables are tender. Place the fish and lemon in a casserole dish and sprinkle with dill. Add the potatoes and vegetables, placing them around the fish. Cover and bake for 10 minutes or until the fish flakes apart. Serves 4.

Tuna and Zucchini Melts

1 can tuna, drained
1/2 cup mayonnaise
1/4 cup finely chopped celery
1/4 cup shredded zucchini
2 green onions, thinly sliced
1 teaspoon prepared mustard
1/4 cup shredded cheddar cheese
4 English muffins, split and toasted
8 tomato slices

Heat oven on broil. In a medium bowl combine the tuna, mayo, celery, zucchini, onion and mustard. Add the cheese and mix. Place the English muffins on a broiling pan and add 1/4 cup of the tuna mixture to each muffin. Broil for 4 minutes or until heated through. Top with a tomato slice and broil for another 1 to 2 minutes.

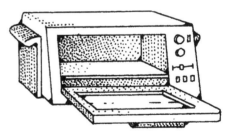

JUST VEGETABLES

Learn to listen. Opportunity sometimes
knocks very softly.

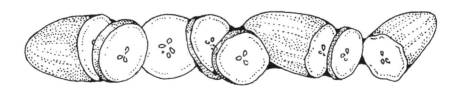

Baked Zucchini Casserole

2-1/2 cups cooked zucchini
1 cup chopped onion
1 green pepper, chopped
3 tablespoons butter
1 cup cooked rice
6 eggs, slightly beaten
salt and pepper to taste
2 cups buttered bread crumbs
1/2 cup mild cheese, grated

Preheat oven to 350°. Sauté the onion and green pepper in butter until tender. Add the zucchini and rice and mix. Place mixture in a casserole dish and mix with the eggs, salt and pepper. Cover with bread crumbs and cheese. Bake in oven for 30 minutes or until eggs are cooked. Serves 6.

Zucchini Pancake

4 or 5 medium zucchini, sliced thin
5 tablespoons salad oil
1 medium onion, chopped
1 green pepper, chopped (optional)
1 tablespoon dry parsley flakes
1 8 ounce can tomato sauce
1 teaspoon basil

1 teaspoon oregano
5 eggs
1/2 cup milk
salt and pepper to taste
3/4 cup grated cheddar cheese
paprika

Warm the oil in an ovenproof skillet. Add the zucchini, onion, green pepper and parsley, cooking until the zucchini is lightly browned and wilted. Reduce heat to low, add the tomato sauce, basil and oregano, simmering until the mixture is moist but not soupy. Combine the eggs, milk, salt and pepper in a small bowl and pour over hot zucchini mixture. Cover and cook over low heat until the eggs begin to set. Sprinkle with grated cheese and paprika. Place under the broiler until the cheese is melted and lightly browned. Cut into wedges and serve. Serves 6 to 8.

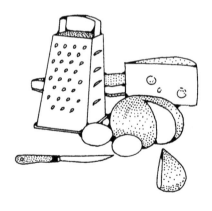

Greek Zucchini and Onion Pizza

1 prepared pizza crust
1 tablespoon olive oil
1 medium onion, thinly sliced
1 medium zucchini, sliced in 1 inch slices
4 or 5 fresh mushrooms, sliced
8 cherry tomatoes, quartered
1 teaspoon Italian seasoning
1 tablespoon crushed fresh garlic
1/4 cup crumbled feta cheese
1/4 cup mozzarella cheese, shredded

Preheat oven to 450°. Warm the olive oil in a large skillet, over medium heat. Add the onion, zucchini, mushrooms, and garlic, sautéing until tender. Toss in the tomatoes for 1 minute and add the seasoning. Spread the mixture over the pizza crust, top with cheese and bake for 8 minutes or until cheese is melted.

Zucchini Fritters

2 tablespoons flour
3 eggs, lightly beaten
salt and pepper to taste
2 cups grated zucchini
2 shallots, finely chopped
2 tablespoons fresh parsley, chopped
sour cream

In a medium sized mixing bowl, combine the flour, eggs, salt and pepper. Add the zucchini, shallots and parsley and mix well. Heat 1/8 of a cup of vegetable oil in a large skillet. Drop the mixture, by tablespoons, into the hot oil. Cook until each side is golden brown and drain on paper towels. Makes about 30 fritters. Serve hot with sour cream.

Steamed Whole Baby Zucchini

1 pound baby zucchini
2 tablespoons unsalted butter
salt and pepper to taste

Place baby zucchini over boiling water for 3 minutes or until just tender. Remove, cool slightly and cut into quarters. Melt butter in a large skillet, add the zucchini and seasoning, tossing gently until heated through. Serves 4.

Stewed Zucchini

1/3 cup olive oil
3 cups coarsely chopped onions
2 medium zucchini, cut into 1/4 inch cubes
2 large green peppers, chopped
2 teaspoons salt
4 medium tomatoes, peeled, seeded and chopped
1 egg, lightly beaten

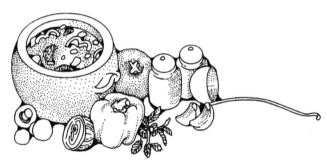

Heat olive oil in a 12 inch skillet over high heat. Add the onions, zucchini, peppers and salt, stirring to combine. Cover and reduce the heat as low as possible. Cook for approximately 40 minutes, stirring occasionally. While zucchini mixture is cooking, place the tomatoes in a saucepan of water. Bring to a boil over medium heat until soft. Puree the tomatoes, by stirring or mashing, and combine with the zucchini mixture. Add the beaten egg, stirring constantly, and simmer for 10 seconds. Do not let mixture boil. Serves 4.

Skillet Squash au Gratin

1/4 cup butter or margarine
4 cups thinly sliced zucchini
1 medium onion, sliced
1 teaspoon salt
dash of pepper
2 peeled and sliced tomatoes
1/2 cup grated American cheese

Melt butter in a large skillet over medium heat. Add squash, onion, salt, pepper and tomatoes. Cover and cook for 10 to 15 minutes, or until squash is tender. Sprinkle with cheese and serve. Serves 4 to 6.

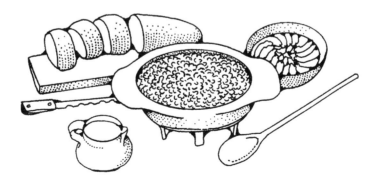

Curried Zucchini Squash

4 small zucchini
3/4 cup thinly sliced onion
2 tablespoons butter or margarine
1/4 teaspoon salt
1/2 teaspoon curry powder
1/8 teaspoon ground black pepper
1 teaspoon fresh lemon juice

Slice the zucchini into 1/4 inch slices. Place zucchini and remaining ingredients in a saucepan over low heat. Cover and cook slowly for 15 minutes or until zucchini is tender. Serve hot. Serves 6.

Zucchini Milano

2 tablespoons butter *(You can't believe)*
1/4 cup chopped onion
1/4 cup chopped green pepper
1/4 teaspoon oregano
4 cups zucchini, sliced 1/4 inch thick
1 tomato, cut into wedges
1 cup shredded cheddar cheese. *(Lo-fat)*

In a large skillet over medium heat, melt the butter. Add the onion, green pepper and oregano, sautéing until tender. Add the zucchini and cover. Cook over low heat for 15 minutes or until the zucchini is tender. Add the tomato and cheese, stirring until the cheese is melted. Serves 6.

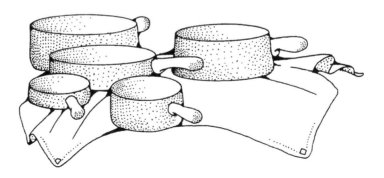

Baked Zucchini in Sour Cream

6 small zucchini, sliced in 1/2 inch slices
2/3 cup sour cream
1 cup grated cheddar cheese
1 tablespoon butter
1/2 teaspoon salt
3 tablespoons fresh bread crumbs
2 tablespoons grated parmesan cheese

Preheat oven to 375°. In a medium saucepan, cover zucchini in water and simmer for 10 minutes. Drain and place in a 8 inch casserole dish. Combine the sour cream, cheddar cheese, butter and salt in a saucepan and heat until blended, stirring with a wire whisk. Pour mixture over zucchini. Combine bread crumbs and remaining cheese, sprinkle over casserole. Bake for 10 minutes and let stand for 5 minutes before serving. Serves 6.

Fried Zucchini

1 medium zucchini, sliced in 1/4 inch slices
2 eggs, beaten
1 cup bread crumbs or more
1/2 teaspoon garlic powder
2 teaspoons Italian seasonings
2 tablespoons grated parmesan cheese
butter flavor Crisco shortening

Place the bread crumbs, garlic, Italian seasoning and cheese in a plastic bag and shake until well mixed. Melt the shortening in a skillet over medium heat, using enough shortening so there is a quarter inch of melted shortening on the bottom of the pan. Dip zucchini in egg and coat with the bread crumb mixture. Fry until tender and brown, turning frequently. Drain on paper towel and serve.

Easy Bean Vegetable Medley

3 tablespoons olive oil
2 large cloves garlic, finely chopped
1 medium eggplant, cut into 1/2 inch pieces
1 large green pepper, cut into 1/2 inch pieces
1 medium zucchini, coarsely chopped
1 can (14 to 16 ounces) whole peeled tomatoes, undrained and chopped
1 envelope Lipton onion soup mix
1 cup water
1 - 16 ounce can cannellini or white kidney beans, rinsed and drained

In a 6 quart saucepan, heat oil over medium heat. Cook eggplant and garlic, stirring occasionally, for 5 minutes. Stir in green pepper, zucchini and tomatoes. Combine the soup mix with one cup of water and add. Bring to a boil, reduce heat and simmer, covered for 25 minutes or until vegetables are tender. Stir in the beans and heat. Makes 5 servings.

Zucchini with Walnuts

3 medium zucchini, sliced into 1 inch slices
5 tablespoons butter
1/2 cup chopped walnuts
salt and pepper to taste

Heat butter in a large skillet over medium heat. Add the zucchini and sauté until zucchini begins to get soft. Meanwhile in a small frying pan, over medium-high heat, melt 2 tablespoons of butter and brown the walnuts. Combine the browned walnuts with the zucchini, salt and pepper. Cook until zucchini is tender, stirring often. Serves 4.

Zucchini in Cream and Chilies

2 medium zucchini, diced
2 medium tomatoes, peeled, diced and seeded
6 peppercorns
2 teaspoons chopped coriander
1 teaspoon chopped mint
1/2 inch cinnamon stick
4 whole cloves
2 whole serrano chili peppers
1/2 cup light cream
salt

Place all ingredients in a medium, non-stick saucepan, over low heat. Cover the pan tightly and cook for 30 minutes, stirring occasionally. If there is not enough liquid in the pan, add a little water. The zucchini is done when it becomes very soft, the cream is completely absorbed and there is no liquid remaining in the pan. The chilies should remain whole and just flavor the zucchini. The dish should not be spicy hot.

Zucchini with Sun-Dried Tomatoes

3 small zucchini, sliced in 1/4 inch slices
4 sun-dried tomatoes in oil
3 - 4 sprigs of fresh rosemary
coarse kosher salt
fresh ground pepper

In a large skillet, heat 2 tablespoons of oil from the tomatoes, over high heat. Sauté squash until lightly browned. Add tomato strips, rosemary, salt and pepper. Toss well and serve hot. Serves 4.

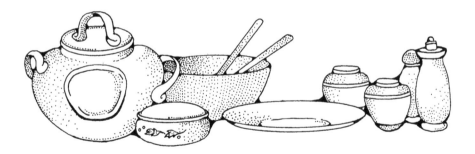

Sautéed Grated Zucchini

2 tablespoons butter
1 small garlic clove, minced
3 medium grated zucchini
salt and pepper to taste
dash of nutmeg (optional)

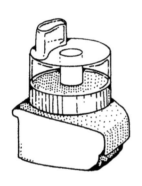

In a large skillet over medium heat, melt the butter. Sauté the garlic for 3 minutes and add the zucchini. Cook for 2 to 3 minutes and season with salt, pepper and nutmeg. Serves 4.

Caraway Summer Squash

1/4 cup nonfat plain yogurt
1 teaspoon cornstarch
2 tablespoons skim milk
1/4 teaspoon caraway seeds
1/8 teaspoon dry mustard
pepper to taste
2 cups zucchini squash, sliced 1/4 inch thick
1 cup halved fresh mushrooms

Mix the yogurt and cornstarch together in a small bowl. Stir in the milk, caraway seeds, mustard and pepper and set aside. In a non-stick skillet, over medium-high heat, add a small amount of oil. Add the zucchini and cook for 2 minutes, add the mush-rooms and cook another 2 to 3 minutes, until crisp-tender. Stir in yogurt mixture and cook, stirring until it thickens and gently begins to boil. Cook for 2 minutes, stirring constantly.

Zucchini in a Half Shell

6 small zucchini, ends trimmed, cut lengthwise
1/4 cup butter
1 tablespoon grated onion
1 beef bouillon cube, crushed
2 tablespoons water

In a large skillet over medium heat, melt the butter. Add the onion, bouillon and water and mix well. Lower heat to simmer and add zucchini, cut side down. Cook until zucchini is golden, adding more water if needed. Cover and cook 10 minutes until tender. Serves 6.

Zucchini and Fresh Herbs

1 tablespoon unsalted butter ("You can't alter")
2 tablespoons olive oil
1 shallot, finely chopped
5 small zucchini, sliced into long julienne slices
1/4 cup fresh chopped parsley
2 sprigs of fresh thyme
salt and pepper

In a large frying pan over medium heat, melt the butter. Add the olive oil and sauté the shallot until tender. Add the zucchini and cook for 3 minutes. Add seasonings and herbs, tossing gently until well mixed. Serves 4.

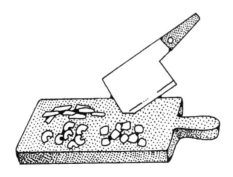

Fresh Tomato Sauce and Zucchini

1 tablespoon butter
1 small onion, sliced thin
4 Roma tomatoes, chopped
2 tablespoons chopped parsley
1/2 teaspoon dried oregano
1/4 teaspoon dried marjoram
salt and pepper
1/8 teaspoon sugar
1-1/2 cups zucchini, sliced in 1/4 inch slices
2 to 4 tablespoons grated mozzarella cheese  (NON-FAT PARMESAN)

Melt butter in a large skillet over medium heat. Add onion, cooking until tender, stir in the tomatoes, parsley, oregano, marjoram, salt, pepper and sugar. Cook an additional 2 minutes, stirring occasionally. Add zucchini and cover, cooking for 4 to 5 minutes or until zucchini is crisp-tender. Sprinkle with cheese and serve. Serves 4.

Braised Zucchini

3 pounds zucchini
2 tablespoons salt
1/3 cup flour
3 tablespoons olive oil
3 tablespoons butter
1/2 cup broth
1/4 teaspoon pepper

Cut zucchini into very thin slices and place in a bowl. Sprinkle with salt and let stand for 30 minutes, stirring occasionally. Drain, dry thoroughly on paper towels, and coat with flour. Heat the oil and butter in a large skillet. Add the floured zucchini and cook until lightly browned. Add the broth and pepper, cover and simmer for 15 minutes or until the zucchini is tender but still crisp. Serves 6 to 8.

Zucchini in Butter

2 to 2-1/2 pounds small zucchini
1/4 cup water
8 tablespoons butter
salt and pepper to taste
2 tablespoons chopped fresh parsley
2 teaspoons fresh lemon juice

In a medium saucepan, place the zucchini, water, butter, salt and pepper. Cover and cook over low heat. Stir frequently, until zucchini is almost soft. Place in a serving dish, sprinkle with parsley and lemon juice and serve.

Zucchini Julienne

4 small zucchini, cut into julienne strips
2 tablespoons unsalted butter
salt and pepper to taste

Steam zucchini in boiling water until tender, about 2 minutes. Drain and add butter, salt and pepper and serve. Serves 4.

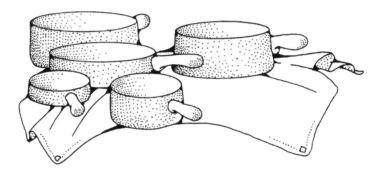

Sautéed Summer Squash

2 small zucchini, thinly sliced
3 tablespoons olive oil
2 cloves of garlic
salt
fresh ground pepper
1 tablespoon cider vinegar
1/4 cup finely chopped fresh parsley or basil

Heat oil in a deep skillet over medium-high heat. Add garlic; when cloves turn a golden brown, remove. Add squash, salt and pepper. Cook 3 to 5 minutes, until tender, but still crisp. Stir in vinegar with herbs and cook 30 seconds longer. Serves 4 to 6.

Zucchini Parmesan

3 cups sliced zucchini
2 tablespoons butter
1/2 teaspoon salt
dash of pepper
2 to 4 tablespoons grated parmesan cheese

In a skillet over medium heat, heat butter. Sauté zucchini, salt and pepper for around 5 minutes covered. Uncover and cook for another 5 minutes, turning slices. Remove from heat and sprinkle with cheese. Serves 4.

Creole Zucchini in a Crock Pot

2 pounds zucchini, sliced in 1/4 inch slices
1 small green pepper, chopped
1 small onion, chopped
1 clove garlic, minced
4 tomatoes, peeled and chopped
1 teaspoon salt
1/4 teaspoon pepper
2 tablespoons butter
2 tablespoons parsley, chopped

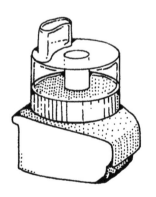

Combine zucchini, green pepper, onion, garlic, salt and pepper in a crock pot. Top with chopped tomatoes and butter. Cover and cook on high for 2 hours or until tender. Sprinkle with chopped parsley. 6 to 7 servings.

Oven Roasted Cheese Vegetables

2 medium russet potatoes
2 medium carrots
1 tablespoon olive oil
1 teaspoon basil
1 teaspoon oregano
salt and pepper to taste
1 large zucchini
1/2 each of a green, yellow and red bell pepper
2 cloves minced garlic
1/2 cup colby cheese, shredded
1/2 cup Monterey jack cheese, shredded
1 cup sharp cheese, shredded

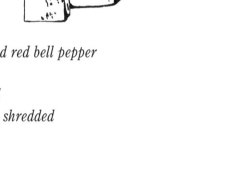

Preheat oven to 425°. Peel potatoes and cut into 1-inch pieces. Peel carrots and cut into 1/2 inch pieces. Place in a 9x13 baking dish and drizzle with olive oil. Sprinkle with basil, oregano, salt and pepper and toss to coat. Bake for 20 minutes. While this is baking, slice the zucchini into 1/2 inch pieces and the peppers into 1 inch pieces. Add zucchini, peppers and garlic to the potato mixture. Stir and return to oven for 20 minutes. Sprinkle with cheese and bake until cheese is melted. Serves 6.

Zucchini in Cheese Sauce

3 small zucchini
salt
1/4 cup milk
1 egg
2/3 cup grated cheese
4 tablespoons butter

Preheat the oven to 400°. Cut zucchini crosswise, then into 1/2 inch slices. Cook in salted water until soft. Beat the egg in a small bowl, add the milk and cheese and stir. Place zucchini in a casserole dish and pour the cheese sauce over it. Dot the top with butter and bake, uncovered, until the cheese is melted and the top is nicely browned. Serves 4.

Baked Zucchini Parmesan

4 to 5 small zucchini, thinly sliced
2 tablespoons butter
1/2 teaspoon salt
dash of pepper
1 cup stewed tomatoes
2 tablespoons grated parmesan cheese

Preheat oven to 350°. Combine the zucchini, butter, seasoning and tomatoes in a casserole dish. Bake for 20 minutes or until zucchini is tender. Sprinkle with cheese and bake 10 minutes longer. Serves 4.

Baked Zucchini

6 small zucchini

3 eggs

5 scallions, chopped, including the
  greens

1/2 cup fresh dill, chopped

1/2 cup fresh mint, chopped

1/2 cup fresh parsley, chopped

1 cup grated gruyére cheese

1/2 cup feta or ricotta cheese

1-1/2 cup flour

salt, pepper and cayenne pepper to taste

4 tablespoons butter

10 pitted black olives (optional)

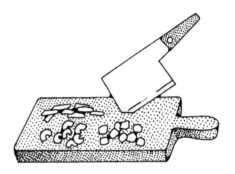

Preheat oven to 350°. Grate zucchini into a large bowl. Mixing well, add the eggs, scallions, herbs and cheese. Add the flour, a little at a time, mixing well each time. Season to taste with salt, pepper and cayenne pepper. Spread mixture evenly in a greased 9 inch square baking dish. Top with black olives and dot with butter. Bake for 45 to 55 minutes or until browned. Cut into squares, serve hot or cold. Serves 6 to 8.

Zucchini and Chili Casserole

3 pounds zucchini, thinly sliced
1 medium white or yellow onion, chopped
1 medium or large can tomato sauce
1 tablespoon bacon fat
1/2 teaspoon salt
3 to 4 dried chili peppers, crushed
1 teaspoon chili powder
1 cup grated cheese (your choice)
1/4 cup cracker crumbs

Preheat oven to 350°. Combine zucchini, onion, tomato sauce and bacon fat in sauce pan. Bring to a boil and simmer for 20 minutes or until tender. Remove from heat and add seasonings. In a 2 quart casserole dish, alternate layers of squash mixture and cheese. Sprinkle with cracker crumbs and bake for 30 minutes. Serves 6 to 8.

Zucchini and Olive Casserole

1-1/2 pounds zucchini, sliced
2 eggs, well beaten
1 teaspoon salt
1/2 cup milk
2 tablespoons grated onion
1 cup dry bread crumbs
1 cup grated American cheese
1/2 cup diced ripe olives

Preheat oven to 350°. Simmer zucchini until tender. Drain. Combine remaining ingredients in a bowl. Stir in zucchini and pour into a buttered casserole dish. Bake for 35 minutes. Serves 6.

Baked Zucchini Squash

3 or 4 small zucchini, chopped
1/4 cup salad oil
1 teaspoon salt
dash of pepper
garlic salt to taste
1 small can of evaporated milk
1 egg
1 slice of bread, crumbled
1 cup grated cheese

Preheat oven to 350°. In a medium saucepan, combine squash, oil, salt and garlic salt with a small amount of water. Cook for 10 minutes. Combine milk and egg in a mixing bowl and beat until blended. Add bread crumbs and let stand until mixture is absorbed into the bread  crumbs. In a 9 or 10 inch casserole dish, place 1/2 of the squash mixture, 1/2 cup of cheese, and one half of the milk mixture. Repeat layers and bake for 45 minutes. Serves 5.

Stuffed Zucchini in a Hurry

Preheat oven to 325°. Take your favorite stuffing recipe or use any boxed stuffing and prepare. Depending on the quantity of stuffing, take a medium to large zucchini and cut in half lengthwise. Hollow out the seeds and lightly coat with margarine. Fill the hollow part of the squash with stuffing. Bake for 30 to 45 minutes or until squash is tender. You may want to place tin foil over the squash to keep the stuffing moist. Serve with any meat.

Stuffed Zucchini

3 medium zucchini, unpeeled
2 tablespoons butter
1/4 pound fresh chopped mushrooms
2 tablespoons flour
1/2 teaspoon salt
1/4 teaspoon oregano
1 cup shredded Monterey jack cheese
2 tablespoons sour cream
1/4 cup parmesan cheese

Cook zucchini in boiling, salted water, covered for 10 to 12 minutes. Drain and cut in half lengthwise. Scoop out the center and chop, leaving 1/4 inch thick shell. In a skillet, melt the butter, sauté the mushrooms and stir in 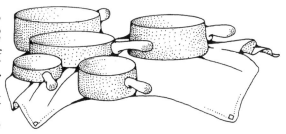 the flour, salt and oregano. Remove from heat. Stir in the cheese, sour cream and zucchini. Fill shells, using about 1/4 cup filling for each one. Top with parmesan cheese and broil until hot and bubbly, about 3 to 5 minutes.

Corn Stuffed Zucchini

3 or 4 medium zucchini
1/4 cup chopped onion
1 tablespoon butter
2 slightly beaten eggs
1 - 8 ounce can whole kernel corn, drained
1/2 cup coarsely crumbled saltine crackers
1/4 cup grated parmesan cheese
1/2 teaspoon salt
a pinch of crushed, dried thyme and garlic
salt and pepper

Preheat oven to 350°. Cut off the ends of the zucchini and cook in boiling water for 5 to 8 minutes. Drain well. Cut in half lengthwise, scoop out centers and chop. In a skillet, over medium heat, melt the butter. Add the onion and cook until tender. Combine the onion with the eggs, corn, cracker crumbs, cheese, chopped squash and seasonings. Mix well. Sprinkle squash shells with salt and spoon in the filling. Place in a baking pan and bake for 30 minutes. You may sprinkle top with more cheese if desired. Serves 6 to 8.

BREADS

God sometimes moves mountains one
pebble at a time.

Zucchini Bread

3 cups flour
1-1/2 cups sugar
2 teaspoons cinnamon
1 teaspoon salt
1/2 teaspoon baking powder
1 teaspoon baking soda
2 cups grated zucchini
1 cup walnuts, chopped
1 cup raisins (optional)
3 eggs
1 cup oil
3 teaspoons vanilla

Preheat oven to 325°. In a mixing bowl, combine all dry ingredients. In a small mixing bowl, beat the eggs, oil and vanilla. Slowly stir into the dry ingredients adding zucchini as you stir. Mix well. Add nuts and raisins. Bake in a loaf pan for 1 hour.

Zucchini Parmesan Bread

3 cups all purpose flour
1 cup peeled, shredded zucchini, drained
1/3 cup sugar
3 tablespoons grated parmesan cheese
1/2 teaspoon baking powder
1/2 teaspoon salt
1 teaspoon baking soda
1/3 cup melted butter
1 cup buttermilk
2 eggs beaten
1 tablespoon grated onion

Preheat oven to 350°. In a bowl mix flour, zucchini, sugar, cheese, baking soda, powder and salt. In another bowl, stir melted butter into the buttermilk. Stir in the eggs and onion. Add this liquid mixture to flour mixture. Batter will be very thick. Mix well. Place in a greased and floured loaf pan. Bake for 1 hour or until done, using toothpick to test.

Zucchini Pineapple Bread

3 eggs	1 teaspoon cinnamon
2 cups sugar	1 cup oil
2 teaspoons vanilla	2 cups flour
1 teaspoon salt	1 teaspoon baking soda
1 cup crushed pineapple	1 teaspoon baking powder
1 cup shredded coconut	1 cup nuts (optional)
2 cups ground zucchini	

Preheat oven to 350°. Combine the eggs, sugar, vanilla and oil, beat well. Stir in the zucchini. In a separate bowl, mix the dry ingredients and slowly fold into the egg mixture. Stir in the pineapple, coconut and nuts. Pour into well greased loaf pans. Makes 2 loaves. Bake for 1 hour.

Whole Wheat Zucchini Bread

3 eggs
2 cups brown sugar
1 cup vegetable oil
3 cups grated zucchini
1 teaspoon vanilla
1 cup whole wheat flour
2 cups white flour
1 teaspoon salt
1 teaspoon baking soda
1/4 teaspoon baking powder
1 teaspoon cinnamon
1 cup nuts

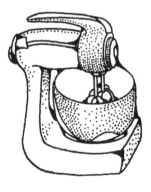

Preheat oven to 350°. Blend eggs, brown sugar, vegetable oil, zucchini and vanilla. In a separate bowl, mix the flour, salt, soda, baking powder and cinnamon. Mix well. Slowly add to the egg mixture. Add nuts and mix. Makes two 5 x 9 inch loaves. Bake in well greased pans for 1 to 1-1/4 hour. Remove from pans when cool. Freezes well.

Zucchini Fruit Bread

3 eggs
1 cup oil
2 cups sugar
2 cups peeled and grated zucchini
1/2 teaspoon vanilla
1/2 teaspoon cinnamon
1 cup chopped walnuts
1/2 teaspoon salt
3 1/2 cups flour
2 teaspoons baking soda
1/2 teaspoon nutmeg
2 cups seedless raisins or currants

Preheat oven to 350°. In a large bowl, mix eggs, sugar and oil. Stir in zucchini. In a separate bowl, mix salt, flour, soda, cinnamon and nutmeg. Slowly add to egg mixture. Mix well and add vanilla. Stir in the nuts and raisins.  Makes two loaves. Bake in well greased and floured loaf pans for 1 to 1-1/4 hour.

DESSERTS

*"Your pain is the breaking of the shell that
encloses your understanding."* Kahlil Gibran

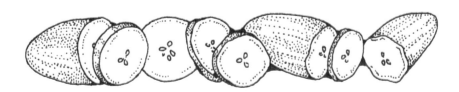

Zucchini and Granola Cookies

3/4 cup butter, softened
1-1/2 cups brown sugar
1 egg
1 teaspoon vanilla
rind of 1 orange, grated
3 cups unpeeled, grated zucchini
3 to 3-1/2 cups flour
1 teaspoon baking soda
1 teaspoon salt
2 cups granola cereal
1 cup butterscotch or chocolate chips

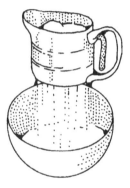

Preheat oven to 350°. Cream butter and sugar in a large mixing bowl. Add the egg, vanilla, orange rind and zucchini. Stir in the flour, soda, salt and granola, mixing well. Stir in the chips. The dough will be real sticky. On a greased cookie sheet, drop cookie dough by small spoonfuls. Bake for 12 to 15 minutes. Cool on rack. Makes 100 cookies.

Zucchini Gem Muffins

3/4 cup flour
1/4 teaspoon baking powder
1/4 teaspoon baking soda
1/4 teaspoon salt
1/4 teaspoon cinnamon
1 egg
1/2 cup sugar
1/4 cup salad oil
1 cup grated zucchini
1/4 cup raisins
1/4 cup chopped walnuts

Preheat oven to 350°. Sift together the flour, baking soda, baking powder, salt and cinnamon. In a separate medium bowl, beat together the egg, sugar and oil until well blended. Add zucchini, raisins and walnuts, stirring well. Stir in dry ingredients, stirring only until dry ingredients are moistened. In a non-stick or greased muffin pan, fill the cups 2/3 full with batter. Bake 25 minutes or until an inserted toothpick comes out clean. Remove from pan. Makes 8 muffins.

Zucchini and Banana Pudding

2 cups unpeeled, cooked zucchini
1 large banana, mashed
2 tablespoons butter or margarine
2 tablespoons sugar
1/2 teaspoon salt
1 egg, beaten

Preheat oven to 350°. Cut zucchini squash in half and remove the seeds. Scoop out the meat part and mash in a bowl. Add the banana, butter, sugar, salt and egg. Mix well. Place mixture in a 1 quart casserole dish and bake for 1 hour or until firm and the top is flecked with brown. Serve hot as a vegetable with pork, ham or poultry. Serves 6.

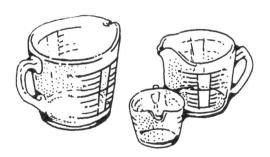

Zucchini Chocolate Bars

3 eggs
2 cups sugar
2 cups grated zucchini
1/2 cup cocoa
2-1/4 cups flour
1 teaspoon baking soda
1 cup and 1 teaspoon vegetable oil
1 tablespoon white vinegar

Preheat oven to 350°. In a mixing bowl, beat the eggs and stir in the oil and the 2 cups sugar slowly. Add the zucchini and mix. In a separate bowl, mix the cocoa, flour and soda. Add this to the egg mixture, stirring until well mixed. Add the vinegar, mixing well. Bake in an ungreased 9 x 13 inch pan for 1 hour.

Quick Zucchini Cake

1 box yellow cake mix
4 eggs
1/2 cup vegetable oil
1 teaspoon cinnamon
2 cups unpeeled, grated zucchini
1/2 cup raisins
1/2 cup chopped walnuts
1 tablespoon vanilla
confectioner's sugar

Preheat oven to 350°. Combine the cake mix, eggs, oil, cinnamon and vanilla in a large bowl and beat for 6 to 7 minutes. Fold in the zucchini, raisins and nuts. Spoon the batter into a greased bundt pan. Bake for 40 to 50 minutes. Test with toothpick for doneness. Remove from pan and cool. Sprinkle with confectioner's sugar.

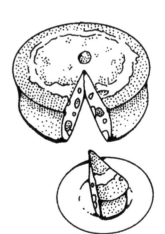

Zucchini Sweeties

1 egg
2 tablespoons margarine
2/3 cup sugar
1-1/2 cups flour
1 teaspoon baking powder
1/3 teaspoon salt
2/3 cup milk
3/4 cup diced zucchini (not shredded)

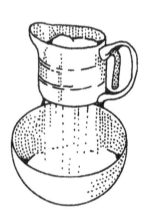

Preheat oven to 350°. In a medium bowl cream the egg, margarine and sugar. In a separate bowl mix the flour, baking powder and salt. Add this slowly to the egg mixture, alternating milk and flour mixture. Mix well and add the diced zucchini. On a greased cookie sheet, spread the mixture very thin. Bake until lightly browned and cake tests done. Take out of oven and turn oven up to 400°.

Top with icing on next page...

Icing

9 tablespoons brown sugar
2 tablespoons cream or milk
4 tablespoons margarine
pinch of salt
1 teaspoon vanilla
1/2 cup chopped nuts
1/2 cup coconut

In a saucepan over low heat cook the sugar, milk and margarine until thick. Add salt, vanilla, coconut and nuts. Pour this over the cake and bake until the top begins to bubble. Remove from oven, cool and cut into squares.

Zucchini Fudge Cake

4 eggs
2-1/4 cups sugar
2 teaspoons vanilla
3/4 cup butter, softened
3 cups flour
1/2 cup unsweetened cocoa
2 teaspoons baking powder
1 teaspoon baking soda
3/4 teaspoon salt
1 cup buttermilk
3 cups shredded zucchini
1 cup walnuts

Preheat oven to 350°. In a large bowl, beat the eggs until fluffy. Add the sugar, beating until mixture is thick and lemon colored. Stir in the vanilla and butter. Combine the flour, cocoa, baking powder, soda and salt in a separate bowl and mix well. Add half of this slowly to egg mixture. Add buttermilk and the other half of the flour mixture. Beat until smooth. Fold in the nuts and zucchini. Pour mixture into 2 round, greased cake pans and bake for 25 to 30 minutes. Cool in pans 10 minutes and remove, cooling completely. *Top with frosting on next page.*

Chocolate Frosting

1 cup butter, softened
2 pounds confectioner's sugar
1/2 cup unsweetened cocoa
1 tablespoon vanilla
1/2 cup milk

Combine all ingredients in a large mixing bowl. Beat on low for 1 minute, then on high until creamy.

Zucchini Cake with Lemon Frosting

2 eggs
1/4 cup milk
2 tablespoons softened butter
1/2 cup sugar
2-1/2 cups Bisquick baking mix
1-1/4 teaspoons cinnamon
3/4 teaspoon nutmeg
1/2 teaspoon ground cloves
2 cups finely shredded zucchini
1 cup raisins
1/2 cup walnuts, chopped

Preheat oven to 350°. Grease and flour a 9 x 9 inch cake pan. Lightly beat eggs, milk, butter and sugar until mixed. In a separate bowl, mix lightly by hand, Bisquick, cinnamon, nutmeg and cloves. Slowly add to the liquid mixture. Mix on low speed for 30 seconds, scraping the bowl constantly. Then beat on medium speed for another 2 minutes, scraping the bowl. Stir in the zucchini, raisins and nuts. Pour batter into pan and bake for 35 to 40 minutes or until wooden toothpick inserted in middle of cake comes out clean. Cool.

Top with frosting on next page.

Lemon Frosting

2 cups powdered sugar
1/4 cup butter or margarine softened
1/2 teaspoon grated lemon peel
2 tablespoons lemon juice

With mixer, blend all ingredients on low speed until mixed. Then beat on medium speed until smooth and fluffy, about 1 minute.

Zucchini Pineapple Cake

1-1/2 cups vegetable oil
3 eggs
2 teaspoons vanilla
2 cups sugar
3 cups flour
2 teaspoons baking soda
1 teaspoon cinnamon
1/2 teaspoon salt
1 small can crushed pineapple
1/2 cup coconut
2 cups ground zucchini
1 cup walnuts, chopped

Preheat oven to 350°. Grease a 9 x 13 inch cake pan. Combine the oil, eggs, vanilla and sugar together. Sift together the flour, soda, cinnamon and salt. Add to the liquid mixture, mixing well. Add the pineapple, coconut, zucchini and walnuts and stir. Pour into cake pan and bake for 1 hour. *Top with frosting on next page.*

Frosting

1 8 ounce package cream cheese
1/2 cup margarine
1 teaspoon vanilla
1 box powdered sugar

Soften the margarine and cream cheese to room temperature. Mix with mixer until creamed. Add the vanilla and powdered sugar and mix well.

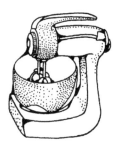

Chocolate Zucchini Cake

1/4 cup margarine
1/2 cup vegetable oil
1 3/4 cups sugar
2 eggs
1/2 cup sour milk
2-1/2 cups flour
4 tablespoons cocoa
1/2 teaspoon baking powder
1 teaspoon baking soda
1/2 teaspoon cinnamon
1/2 teaspoon cloves
2 cups grated zucchini
1/2 cup chocolate chips

Preheat oven to 325°. In a mixing bowl, on medium speed, cream the margarine, oil and sugar together. Add the eggs, vanilla and sour milk and mix well. In another bowl, mix all dry ingredients and add to liquid mixture. Beat well and stir in the zucchini. Pour into a greased 9 x 5 inch loaf pan or 10 x 10 inch cake pan. Sprinkle with chocolate chips and bake for 40 to 50 minutes. Done when wooden toothpick comes out clean. Serve with whipped topping if desired.

INDEX

*Never give up on anybody. Miracles
happen everyday.*

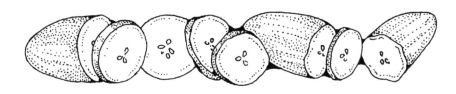

Look for Joan Bestwick's *Life's Little Rhubarb Cookbook* and *Life's Little Berry Cookbook,* also by Avery Color Studios, Inc.

Avery Color Studios, Inc. has a full line of Great Lakes oriented books, cookbooks, puzzles, shipwreck and lighthouse maps, and lighthouse posters.

For a full color catalog call:
1-800-722-9925

Avery Color Studios, Inc. products are available at gift shops and bookstores throughout the Great Lakes region.